JUN   2001

Cornerstones of Freedom

Impeachment

ANDREW SANTELLA

CHILDREN'S PRESS®
A Division of Grolier Publishing
New York • London • Hong Kong • Sydney
Danbury, Connecticut

Visit Children's Press on the Internet at:
http://publishing.grolier.com

Library of Congress Cataloging-in-Publication Data

Santella, Andrew.
Impeachment / Andrew Santella.
    p. cm — (Cornerstones of freedom)
  Includes index.
  Summary: Surveys the history of impeachment in the United States,
discussing the basic rules and procedures and notable officials who have
been impeached.
  ISBN 0-516-21677-5 (lib.bdg.)   0-516-27166-0 (pbk.)
1. Impeachments—United States—Juvenile literature.
[1. Impeachments. 2. United States—Politics and government.]
I. Series.
KF5075.Z9 S26   2000
342.73'068—dc21
                                                99-053184
                                                   CIP
                                                   AC

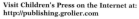

GROLIER
PUBLISHING

©2000 Children's Press®
A Division of Grolier Publishing Co., Inc.
All rights reserved. Published simultaneously in Canada.
Printed in the United States of America.
1 2 3 4 5 6 7 8 9 10 R 09 08 07 06 05 04 03 02 01 00

On March 13, 1868, the chambers of the United States Senate were overflowing. All fifty-four senators were in their seats on the floor of the Senate. The galleries were packed with reporters, diplomats, and other spectators. They were all there to see something that had never happened in the history of the United States— the impeachment trial of a president.

Suddenly, a voice boomed out from the floor of the Senate. "Andrew Johnson, president of the United States! Andrew Johnson, president of the United States! Appear and answer the charges of impeachment exhibited against you by the House of Representatives of the United States."

The U.S. Senate hears the first impeachment case against a president— Andrew Johnson.

So began the impeachment trial of President Andrew Johnson. It lasted for seventy-five days. If the president had been found guilty, he would have had to leave office. But Johnson was not found guilty. When it was all over, one senator said of the trial, "It is to be hoped that its like may never return." Later, however, there would be other impeachment trials. In fact, 131 years later, another president, Bill Clinton, was impeached, stood trial, and found not guilty.

Impeachment is the process by which federal officials are accused of misconduct, tried, and possibly removed from office. Impeachment trials have been rare events in American history. Some, such as the trials of presidents Johnson and Clinton, have divided Americans. But these trials also offer a lesson in the wisdom and the workings of the government created by the men who wrote the Constitution.

The federal government of the United States is divided into three branches—legislative, executive, and judicial. The Constitution assigns specific powers to each branch. The Congress (the House of Representatives and the Senate) heads the legislative branch and passes laws. The president heads the executive branch and is responsible for enforcing those laws. The Supreme Court heads the judicial branch. It decides which laws or acts should be overturned because they are not in keeping with the principles, or rules, of the Constitution.

The Constitution gives Congress the power to impeach. If members of Congress believe that a public official—such as a judge or even a president of the United States—has abused his or her power, Congress can try to impeach that person. The Constitution states that the House of Representatives has the "sole Power of Impeachment." The Senate has "the sole Power to try all Impeachments." In other words, removing officials from office requires two steps. First, the House of Representatives makes a formal accusation, called the Articles of Impeachment, against the official. A majority of the House has to vote in favor of impeachment. Then, the Senate conducts a trial. If two out of every three senators find the official guilty, that person is removed from office. So, an impeachment is the accusation made by the House of Representatives. But impeachment can also mean the whole process that results, including the trial in the Senate.

The power to impeach is one of the most serious responsibilities granted to Congress by the Constitution. Because it is such a serious matter, Congress does not often try to remove officials from their jobs. The House of Representatives has impeached only sixteen officials. Seven of them—all judges—were removed from office after being found guilty by the Senate. The sixteen officials impeached by the House of Representatives include two presidents, a cabinet member (one of the president's advisers), a senator, a Supreme Court justice, and eleven federal judges.

The Constitution defines when impeachment is necessary. It says the "President, Vice President and all civil Officers of the United States shall be removed from Office on Impeachment for, and conviction of, Treason, Bribery, or other high Crimes and Misdemeanors." But experts have different opinions on what that definition means. Treason and bribery are clearly defined. The Constitution says treason means helping the enemies of the United States. Bribery is the acceptance of something valuable in return for corrupt behavior in public duty.

There has always been discussion, however, about what is meant by "high Crimes and Misdemeanors." Some experts on the Constitution say that officials should be impeached and removed from office only for the most serious crimes against the nation. Others insist that officials can be impeached and removed from office for any illegal act.

Although the Constitution does not define "high Crimes and Misdemeanors," it is known that the founders disagreed about what crimes could be punished by impeachment. Original proposals said that a president could be removed from office for "corrupt conduct." Later, that was changed to "Bribery, Treason or Corruption." George Mason of Virginia suggested adding the phrase "other high Crimes and Misdemeanors against the state." The final draft of the Constitution said that officials could be impeached for "Treason, Bribery or other high Crimes and Misdemeanors."

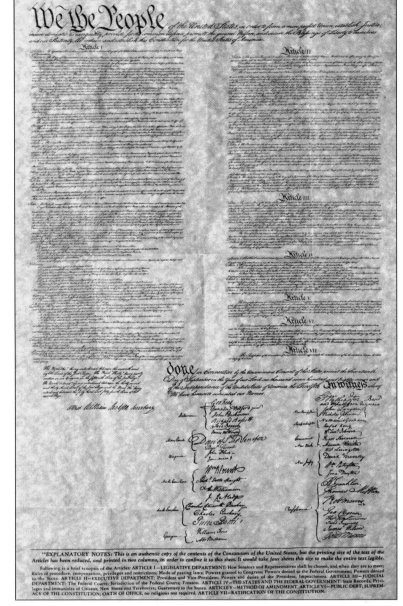

The founders' guidelines for impeachment are found in Article I of the Constitution.

When the Constitution was written, the authors argued over whether or not impeachment was necessary. Some thought giving Congress the power of impeachment would weaken the office of the president. But others, such as James Madison, argued successfully that impeachment would protect against "corruption . . . [that] might be fatal to the republic."

James Madison. Most people consider him to be the "Father of the Constitution."

There was also disagreement about how impeachment trials should be conducted. Some at the convention argued that the Supreme Court should preside over impeachment trials. Others suggested that the chief justices of all the state supreme courts should preside over them. Finally, it was agreed that the Senate would function as a court of law that would conduct impeachment trials. Although the basic rules for impeachment were laid out in the Constitution, it took time and experience to learn how the process would work when tested. The first official impeached by the House of Representatives was Senator William Blount of Tennessee. In 1797, he was accused of a plot to help the British seize Louisiana and Florida from Spain. The Senate dismissed the charges on January 14, 1799. Instead of conducting an impeachment trial, Blount was simply kicked out of the Senate. From then on, legislators (senators and members of the House of Representatives) were considered exempt, or excused, from impeachment.

William Blount. Before he was a senator from Tennessee, he signed the Constitution for North Carolina.

Judge John Pickering of New Hampshire was the first impeached official to be convicted by the Senate. On March 12, 1803, the Senate found him guilty of misconduct and drunkenness. Pickering was removed from office.

The 1805 impeachment of Associate Justice Samuel Chase was one of the first major tests of the impeachment process. Chase was a member of the Federalist Party. The Federalist Party was one of two political parties competing for control of the federal government in the 1790s and early 1800s. The Federalists' rivals in the Democratic Party hoped to take control of the U.S. Supreme Court. They planned to try to impeach leading Federalists on the Court. The Democrats hoped that once the Federalists were removed from the Supreme Court, Democrats could replace them.

Democrats in the House of Representatives charged Chase with making harsh and

John Pickering

unfair rulings. A majority of the members of the House of Representatives voted to impeach Chase. He was then put on trial in the Senate.

Chase's trial in the Senate began on February 9, 1805, and lasted for nearly a month. When the trial was over, there weren't enough votes in the Senate to convict Chase. He was found not guilty, and he remained on the Supreme Court. Many experts believe that if Chase had been found guilty, Democrats in Congress would have impeached other Federal judges. Chase's trial established an important principle: differences in political beliefs should not be the grounds for impeachment.

Samuel Chase, one of the signers of the Declaration of Independence

Since then, officials have been impeached for different crimes, such as bribery, treason, perjury, and cheating on income taxes. But Chase was not the last official to be impeached for political differences. It happened again in 1868, when President Andrew Johnson was impeached.

Johnson had been vice president under Abraham Lincoln at the end of the American Civil War (1861–1865). When Lincoln was assassinated in 1865, Johnson became president. It became his job to reunite the northern and southern states after the long and bloody war. But this task proved to be nearly impossible. Almost as soon as he became president, Johnson had trouble with members of Congress and his own cabinet.

Andrew Johnson was president from 1865 to 1869.

Many members of the Republican Party did not trust Johnson. He was from Tennessee—a Southern state. He had been the only senator from a Southern state to remain loyal to the Union at the start of the Civil War. But at the end of the war, many Republicans wanted to punish the South harshly. They distrusted Southerners, including Johnson.

He also disagreed with a group of the Republican Party, called the Radical Republicans, about how to reunite the nation. They wanted to establish military rule over the South. Johnson wanted to let the Southern states rejoin the Union when they agreed to abolish slavery. The Radical Republicans wanted full civil rights for the newly freed blacks in the South. Johnson tried to veto—or overrule—attempts to protect former slaves. In 1867, Radical Republicans in Congress led the passage of the Tenure of Office Act. This act forbade the president to remove civil officers without the approval of the Senate. It meant that Johnson had to have the Senate's permission to fire his own officers.

Edwin Stanton served under presidents Lincoln and Johnson.

Early in 1868, Johnson decided to ignore the Tenure of Office Act. He dismissed Secretary of War Edwin M. Stanton on February 21—even though the Senate had declared that it would not give him permission. Johnson's actions enraged Congress. Members of the House of Representatives had tried to impeach him before, but they had failed. Now the House voted on Johnson's impeachment once more. This time, it debated for only three days and voted 126–47 to impeach him.

The House drew up eleven articles of impeachment, outlining the charges against Johnson. The main charge was violating the Tenure of Office Act by firing Stanton. On March 6, 1868, the Senate was sworn in as a court to hear the impeachment case. It demanded that the president appear in the Senate a week later to answer the charges.

On March 13, 1868, the sergeant at arms (the officer in charge of preserving order in the Senate) called for the president to appear. The doors to the Senate chamber were thrown open. But Johnson was nowhere to be seen. Instead, his lawyers entered the Senate chamber and asked for more time to prepare their defense of the president.

Questions about how to conduct the trial were still unresolved. The Constitution calls for the vice president to preside over impeachment trials in the Senate—except when the president is on trial. (Since the vice president would be next in line to take over as president, he could not be expected to be a fair judge.) So, in impeachment trials of the president, the Constitution says that the chief justice of the Supreme Court presides.

In Johnson's case, one of the members of the Senate, Benjamin Wade, would become president if Johnson were removed from office. Should Wade be allowed to vote, even though he might not be a fair judge? The Senate decided that he could. It also decided that Johnson's son-in-law, a Senator from Tennessee, could vote.

On March 30, 1868, Johnson's accusers in the House of Representatives (called impeachment managers) began stating their case. The seven managers had to convince the members of the Senate that the president should be removed from office. Their speeches revealed the bitterness of the trial. One of them, George Boutwell, said that Johnson was an accessory (someone who participates without being present) in Lincoln's murder. "By murder most foul he succeeded to the presidency," Benjamin Butler told the Senate, "and is the elect of an assassin to that high office, and not of the people." By linking Johnson to the crime of killing Lincoln, Butler hoped to convince the Senate to impeach the new president.

The Johnson Impeachment Committee

Johnson's lawyers argued in his defense. They said that the president believed he had a right to fire Stanton. They also said that the Tenure of Office Act did not follow the principles of the Constitution. Therefore, the president should not have to follow it. Johnson was a very unpopular president. Newspapers all over the country mocked him. Voters were unhappy with him. And most Republicans in Congress were determined to remove him from office. Most people expected the Senate to convict Johnson. But six Republican senators announced that they would vote to acquit him.

This political cartoon appeared in Harper's Weekly *on March 21, 1868, during President Johnson's impeachment trial. The cartoon depicts the Constitution falling on Johnson and crushing him.*

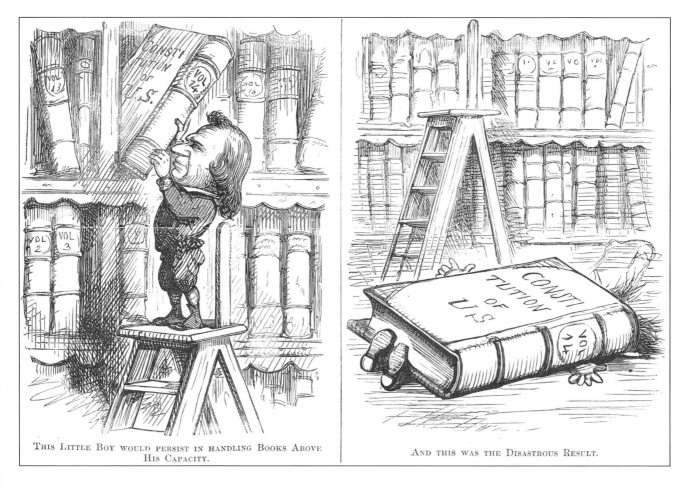

THIS LITTLE BOY WOULD PERSIST IN HANDLING BOOKS ABOVE HIS CAPACITY.

AND THIS WAS THE DISASTROUS RESULT.

Their announcement put pressure on Edmund Ross, a Republican senator from Kansas. He was one of the last senators to declare how he would vote. His vote would decide the president's fate. Ross did not like Johnson. Ross had been warned that a vote to acquit Johnson would end his career. Still, on May 16, 1868, he voted, finding Johnson not guilty. "I almost literally looked down into my open grave," he later wrote. However, Ross believed that in this case, the president was right.

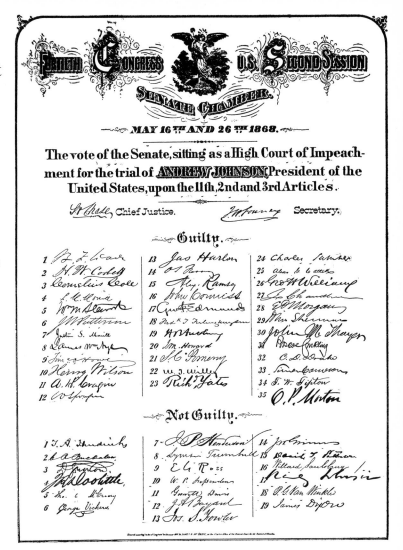

In the impeachment trial of President Johnson, thirty-five senators voted guilty, and nineteen voted not guilty.

Ross's vote saved Johnson. Nineteen senators voted that Johnson was not guilty. Thirty-five voted guilty. That number was one vote short of the total required to convict him. If just one senator had changed his vote, Johnson would have been stripped of the presidency.

Soon after the trial, even congressmen who had wanted to convict Johnson began to think the impeachment had been a mistake. "It was not justifiable on the charges made," said James G. Blaine, who voted for impeachment. He said that convicting Johnson would have done more harm than Johnson himself ever could have done. Senator Lyman Trumbull said that if Johnson had been convicted, no president would "be safe who happens to differ" with Congress. The Tenure of Office Act was partially repealed in 1887. In 1926, the Supreme Court declared the law unconstitutional. Still, for many years after the Johnson impeachment, some people felt that the power of the presidency was weakened.

The next serious challenge to a president did not come for more than one hundred years, but it eventually forced President Richard M. Nixon from office. Nixon's trouble began on June 17, 1972. That day, five men were caught breaking into the offices of the Democratic National Committee in the Watergate apartments in Washington, D.C. Nixon was preparing to run for re-election as the Republican Party's candidate for president. It turned out that Nixon's re-election campaign committee had hired the burglars. They had broken into the offices to hide listening devices to be used for spying. The arrest began a series of events that placed the president in deeper and deeper trouble. The president and his aides tried to cover up their involvement in the break-in. They paid the burglars to keep quiet about their role. They ordered a stop to an investigation of the break-in by the Federal Bureau of Investigation (FBI). The president refused to turn over evidence relating to the case. Nixon fired a special prosecutor investigating the case.

Richard Nixon was the first president to resign from office.

Evidence of the president's wrongdoing became clear, however. In July 1974, the Judiciary Committee of the House of Representatives approved articles of impeachment against Nixon. They accused him of illegal wire-tapping (spying), perjury, bribery, and obstruction of justice. The articles of impeachment claimed, "In all of this, Richard M. Nixon has acted in a manner contrary to his trust as President . . . to the manifest injury of the people of the United States."

It seemed certain that the House of Representatives would impeach Nixon. Nixon chose not to put the country through his impeachment and the trial that would follow. On August 9, 1974, he resigned. Even though there had been no impeachment, the Watergate scandal and Nixon's resignation upset the nation. Senator Sam Ervin called it "the greatest tragedy this country has suffered." After Nixon resigned, Vice President Gerald Ford became president. One month later, Ford pardoned Nixon for any crimes he may have committed, thus excusing him from punishment.

Four years later, Congress enacted the Ethics in Government Act. It gave a special prosecutor the power to investigate accusations against the president. This prosecutor later came to be called an independent counsel. Not even the president could fire an independent counsel. This act was passed because Nixon had fired the official who was investigating him. By firing him, Nixon used his power as president to influence a legal matter that concerned him. The law was designed to prevent something similar from happening again. Under the law, the executive branch would not investigate its own officials. Congress decided to renew the act every five years if it proved helpful.

Across the country, newspapers announced Nixon's resignation.

The New York Times

"All the News That's Fit to Print"

NEW JERSEY EDITION

VOL.CXXIII....No.42,566

— NEW YORK, FRIDAY, AUGUST 9, 1974 —

15 CENTS

NIXON RESIGNS

HE URGES A TIME OF 'HEALING'; FORD WILL TAKE OFFICE TODAY

The 37th President First to Leave Post

By JOHN HERBERS

WASHINGTON, Aug. 8—Richard Milhous Nixon, the 37th President of the United States, announced tonight that he had given up his long and arduous fight to remain in office and would resign, effective at noon tomorrow. Gerald Rudolph Ford, whom Mr. Nixon nominated for Vice President last Oct. 12, will be sworn in tomorrow at the same hour as the 38th President of the United States, to serve out the 895 days remaining in Mr. Nixon's second term.

Less than two years after his landslide election to a second term, Mr. Nixon, in a conciliatory address on national television, said he was leaving not with a sense of bitterness but with a hope his departure would start a "process of healing that is so desperately needed in America."

The 61-year-old Mr. Nixon, appearing calm, became the first President in the history of the Republic to resign from office.

Text of the address will be found on Page 2.

A Speech to Nation Is Expected Tonight

By ANTHONY RIPLEY

WASHINGTON, Aug. 8—Gerald R. Ford, who never sought the nation's highest office, was preparing tonight to become the 38th President of the United States.

Along Pennsylvania Avenue three days ago, history was being enacted, that plans rang out when he appeared. A ceremony is scheduled for noon tomorrow in the East Room of the White House where Mr. Ford is to raise his hand and "solemnly" swear to execute the office of the President and defend the Constitution.

And thus will be become the first man to serve as President without a vote of the American people.

It will be a small private ceremony, attended only by close friends, and it is expected that he will address the nation tomorrow night on radio and television.

Last Oct. 26, as Mr. Ford was returning on a plane from a trip to Ohio when his nomination for Vice President was still under consideration was asked by a reporter asked him, replied you like to be President.

SPECULATION RIFE ON VICE PRESIDENT

Vice President Ford at event for servicemen yesterday

President Nixon on TV as he announced his resignation.

In 1998, Bill Clinton became only the second president in U.S. history to be impeached. Clinton's impeachment grew out of a long investigation of real estate transactions he had made before he was president. In 1994, the Justice Department began to look into them. It wanted to know if money from the transactions had been used improperly for his election campaign. Attorney General Janet Reno appointed an independent counsel, Kenneth Starr, to look into the matter.

Janet Reno, attorney general during the Clinton scandal

During this process, the focus shifted away from Clinton's real estate transactions. Instead, Starr began trying to show that President Clinton had lied under oath about his relationships with women outside his marriage. In January 1998, Starr officially expanded his investigation to include the president's relation-ships. Days later, the president denied that he had had an improper relationship with a young woman working at the

White House named Monica Lewinsky.

Still, questions about President Clinton's behavior continued. A grand jury was appointed to look into the case. A grand jury hears testimony when people are accused of certain crimes. It decides if there is enough evidence to warrant a trial. On August 17, 1998, Clinton testified before the grand jury about his behavior. He was the first president to testify in his own defense before a grand jury. He admitted to the grand jury that he did have an "inappropriate relationship" with Monica Lewinsky. On television later that evening, he told the nation.

Independent Counsel Kenneth Starr

Monica Lewinsky and her spokeswoman, Judy Smith, in Washington, D.C., on July 28, 1998.

In September, Starr sent a detailed report to Congress. It claimed that President Clinton had engaged in "a pattern of . . . lies" to cover up his actions. In December, the Judiciary Committee of the House of Representatives voted in favor of impeaching Clinton. On December 19, 1998, the entire House impeached the president. Two of the articles of impeachment accused him of lying under oath and obstructing justice.

Clinton became the first president since Andrew Johnson to stand trial in the Senate. But the Clinton case was much different than the Johnson case. Although Johnson was extremely unpopular with voters, Clinton's popularity remained strong even after he was impeached. Most Americans approved of the job he was doing as president—even if they disapproved of his personal behavior. Clinton's popularity probably affected the conduct of his trial. Many senators were determined to keep

On December 19, 1998, House Judiciary Chairman Henry Hyde (far right) delivers the Articles of Impeachment against President Clinton to the Secretary of the Senate, Gary Sisco (far left).

the trial short. They did not want to spend too much time trying to impeach a president who was supported by many Americans.

The trial lasted just more than a month. Supreme Court Chief Justice William Rehnquist presided over the trial. On February 12, 1999, the Senate was ready to vote. The sergeant at arms read the articles of impeachment aloud. Then Rehnquist asked, "Senators, how say you? Is the respondent, William Jefferson Clinton, guilty or not guilty?"

Ticket to the opening day of President Clinton's impeachment trial

There were separate votes on each charge against Clinton—perjury and obstruction of justice. To remove him from office, 66 of the 100 senators would have to find the president guilty. Only 45 of the senators found Clinton guilty of perjury. Fifty senators found him guilty of obstruction of justice, and 50 found him not guilty. After the vote was announced, Rehnquist declared: "It is therefore ordered and adjudged that the said William Jefferson Clinton be and hereby is acquitted of the charges in the said articles." The trial was over. Clinton remained president.

On February 12, 1999, Chief Justice William Rehnquist announces the acquittal of President Clinton.

In June 1999, Congress did not renew the Ethics in Government Act. Many people believed the Act caused more problems than it solved. Congress' power to impeach is rarely used. Both of the impeachments of presidents have created divisions among Americans. But impeachment is important to the U.S. government. This process helps ensure that the nation's officials will do their jobs honestly, and it provides a way for the people to remove officials who have betrayed their trust.

President Clinton apologizes to the nation after his impeachment.

FEDERAL OFFICIALS WHO

William Blount
Senator from Tennessee, 1799
Charges dismissed

John Pickering
Judge of the U.S. District Court
for New Hampshire, 1803
Removed from office

Samuel Chase
Associate justice of the
Supreme Court, 1805
Acquitted

James H. Peck
Judge of the U.S. District
Court for Missouri, 1831
Acquitted

West H. Humphreys
Judge of the U.S. District Court for
the middle, eastern, and western
districts of Tennessee, 1862
Removed

Andrew Johnson
Seventeenth president of the
United States, 1868
Acquitted

William W. Belknap
Secretary of war, 1876
Acquitted

Charles Swayne
Judge of the U.S. District Court for
the northern district of Florida, 1905
Acquitted

HAVE BEEN IMPEACHED

Robert W. Archbald
Associate judge, U.S. Commerce
Court, 1913
Removed from office

George W. English
Judge of the U.S. District Court for
the eastern district of Illinois, 1926
Resigned

Harold Louderback
Judge of the U.S. District Court
for the northern district of
California, 1933
Acquitted

Halsted L. Ritter
Judge of the U.S. District Court
for the southern district of
Florida, 1936
Removed from office

Harry E. Claiborne
Judge of the U.S. District Court
for the district of Nevada, 1986
Removed from office

Alcee L. Hastings
Judge of the U.S. District Court
for the southern district of
Florida, 1988
Removed from office

Walter L. Nixon
Judge of the U.S. District Court
for Mississippi, 1989
Removed from office

William J. Clinton
Forty-second president of the
United States, 1998
Acquitted

GLOSSARY

accusation – a statement that a person is guilty of wrongdoing

acquit – to state in an official way that a person is innocent of a crime or wrongdoing

attorney general – the chief law officer of a nation or state who represents the government in legal cases and serves as its principal legal adviser

civil rights – individual rights that all members of a society have to freedom and equal treatment under the law

Janet Reno, attorney general during the Clinton scandal

conviction – the process of finding or proving a person guilty

corrupt – evil or wicked

independent counsel – a lawyer who investigates accusations against the president

misdemeanor – a criminal offense

obstruction of justice – to block or hinder the carrying out of the law

perjury – lying when swearing to tell the truth under oath in a court of law

prosecutor – a person who heads an investigation before a court

real estate – land or buildings that make up property

repeal – to do away with officially

Independent Counsel Kenneth Starr

testimony – a statement made under oath; proof

transaction – an exchange of goods and services

warrant – to call for; deserve

TIMELINE

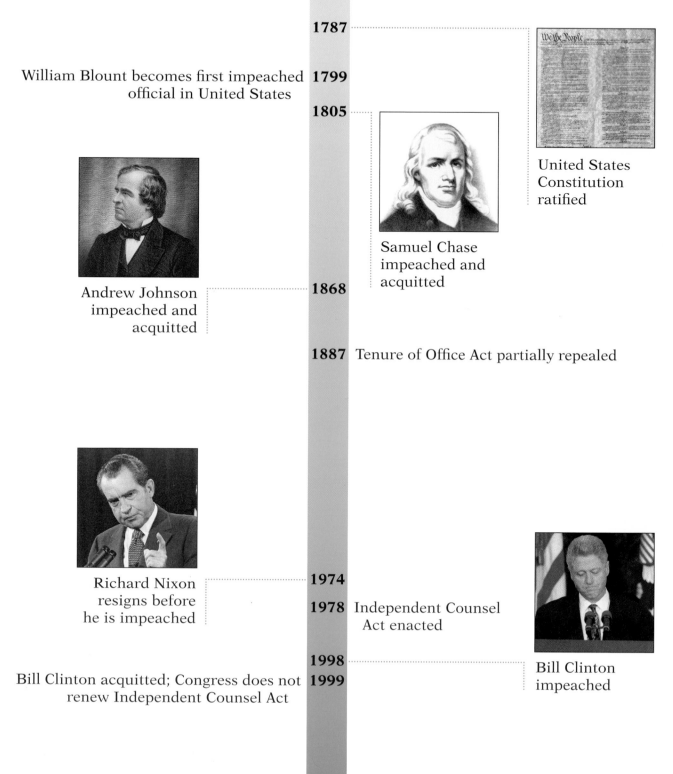

1787 .... United States Constitution ratified

William Blount becomes first impeached **1799**
official in United States

1805 .... Samuel Chase impeached and acquitted

Andrew Johnson impeached and acquitted **1868**

1887 Tenure of Office Act partially repealed

Richard Nixon resigns before he is impeached **1974**

1978 Independent Counsel Act enacted

1998 .... Bill Clinton impeached

Bill Clinton acquitted; Congress does not **1999**
renew Independent Counsel Act

INDEX (*Boldface* page numbers indicate illustrations.)

Archbald, Robert W., 29
articles of impeachment, 5, 14, 20, 24, 25
Belknap, William W., 28
Blaine, James G., 18
Blount, William, 9, **9**, 28, **28**
Boutwell, George, 15
Chase, Samuel, 10–11, **11**, 28, **28**
Civil War, 12
Claiborne, Harry E., 29
Clinton, William J. (Bill), 4, 22–26, 27, 29, **29**
Congress, U.S., 4, 6, 13, 20, 21
Constitution, 4, 5, **5**, 6, 7, 8, 9, 14, 16
Democratic Party, 10, 11
English, George W., 29
Ervin, Sam, 20
Ethics in Government Act, 20–21, 27
Federal Bureau of Investigation (FBI), 19
Federalist Party, 10, 11

Ford, Gerald, 20
grand jury, 23
Hastings, Alcee L., 29
high crimes and misdemeanors, 6–8
House of Representatives, 4, 5, 6, 9, 10, 13, 15, 20, 24
Humphreys, West H., 28
impeachment managers, 15, **15**
independent counsel, 20–21, 22, 27
Johnson, Andrew, **3**, 3–4, 11–12, **12**, 13–17, **16**, 24, 27, 28, **28**
Judiciary Committee of House of Representatives, 20, 24
Lewisky, Monica, 23, **24**
Lincoln, Abraham, 12, 15
Louderback, Harold, 29
Madison, James, 8, **8**
Mason, George, 8
Nixon, Richard M., 18–19, **19**, 20–21
Nixon, Walter L., 29

Peck, James H., 28
Pickering, John, 10, **10**, 28, **28**
Radical Republicans, 12–13
Rehnquist, William, 25, 26
Reno, Janet, 22, **22**
Republican Party, 12, 16, 18
Ritter, Halsted L., 29
Ross, Edmund, 17
Senate, U.S., 3, 4, 5, 8, 9, 14–15, 16
sergeant at arms, 14
Stanton, Edwin, 13, **13**, 14, 16
Starr, Kenneth, 22, **23**, 24
Supreme Court, U.S., 4, 8, 10, 14, 18, 25
Swayne, Charles, 28
Tenure of Office Act, 13, 14, 16, 18
Trumbull, Lyman, 18
Wade, Benjamin, 14
Watergate, 18

PHOTO CREDITS

Photographs ©: AP/Wide World Photos: 22 (Doug Mills); Archive Photos: 1, 23, 30 top (CNP), 25 top (Larry Downing), 13, 16, 21; Corbis-Bettmann: 19, 31 bottom left (UPI), cover, 2, 27, 29, 31 bottom right; Jay Mallin: 25 bottom; Liaison Agency, Inc.: 24 (George DeKeerle), 5 (Hulton Getty), 26 (Liaison Pool); New Hampshire Historical Society: 10, 28 top right; North Wind Picture Archives: 8, 11, 28 bottom left, 31 top right; Stock Montage, Inc.: 3, 12, 15, 17, 28 bottom right, 30 bottom, 31 top left; Superstock, Inc.: 7, 31 top far right; Tennessee State Library and Archives: 9, 28 top left.

PICTURE IDENTIFICATIONS

Cover photo: President Bill Clinton at the White House after he was impeached
Page 1: The U.S. Senate votes on the articles of impeachment against President Bill Clinton. Chief Justice William Rehnquist is presiding.
Page 2: The Capitol, where Congress works and impeachment trials take place

ABOUT THE AUTHOR

Andrew Santella lives in Chicago. He writes for magazines, including *GQ*, *Nickelodeon*, and *Commonweal*. Mr. Santella is also the author of several books for Children's Press: *The Capitol*, *The Chisholm Trail*, *Illinois*, and *Thomas Jefferson: Voice of Liberty*.